A Visit to
IRELAND

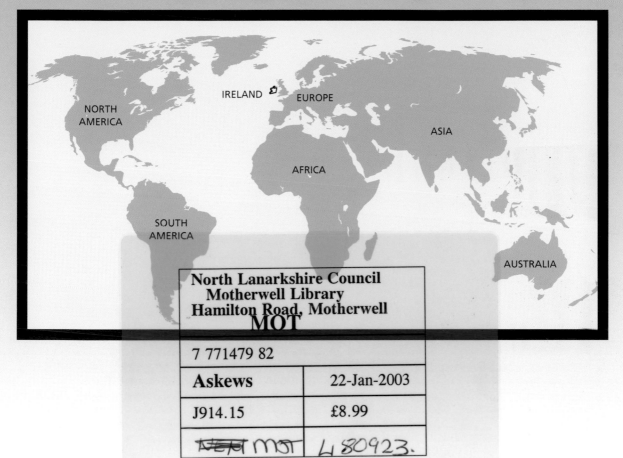

IRELAND
NORTH AMERICA
EUROPE
ASIA
AFRICA
SOUTH AMERICA
AUSTRALIA

Rachael Bell

Heinemann
LIBRARY

First published in Great Britain by Heinemann Library,
Halley Court, Jordan Hill, Oxford OX2 8EJ,
a division of Reed Educational and Professional Publishing Ltd.

Heinemann is a registered trademark of Reed Educational & Professional Publishing Limited.

OXFORD MELBOURNE AUCKLAND
JOHANNESBURG BLANTYRE GABORONE
IBADAN PORTSMOUTH (NH) USA CHICAGO

Designed by AMR
Illustrations by Art Construction
Printed and bound in Hong Kong/China by South China Printing Co.

03 02 01 00
10 9 8 7 6 5 4 3 2

ISBN 0 431 08341 X

British Library Cataloguing in Publication Data

Bell, Rachael
  A visit to Ireland
  1. Ireland – Juvenile literature
  I.Title II.Ireland
  941.5

Acknowledgements
The Publishers would like to thank the following for permission to reproduce photographs:
Brian Kelly p 23; Collections: Michael Diggin p 6, George Wright pp 10, 13, Michael St Maursheil
pp 14, 20, 25; Hutchison Library: P. Moszynski p 21; Images Colour Library: pp 7, 26; Image Ireland:
Alain Le Garsmeur pp 8, 19, Geray Sweeney p 18; J. Allan Cash Ltd: pp 9, 16; Photo Images Ltd:
pp 11, 24, 27; Rex Features London: Steve Wood p 15; Robert Harding Picture Library: Duncan
Maxwell p 17; The Bridgeman Art Library: Board of Trinity College Dublin p 28; Tony Stone
Worldwide: Oliver Benn p 5; The Slide File: pp 12, 22, 29.

Cover photograph reproduced with permission of Tony Stone Images/John Fortunato.

Every effort has been made to contact copyright holders of any material reproduced in this
book. Any omissions will be rectified in subsequent printings if notice is given to the Publisher.

Any words appearing in bold, **like this**, are explained in the Glossary.

Contents

Ireland

Key
- Land above 0m/sea level
- Land over 500m
- Capital ●
- Important cities ●
- R. River

(Map labels: North, NORTHERN IRELAND, THE UNITED KINGDOM, Donegal, R. Boyne, Dublin, R. Liffey, IRISH SEA, Galway, ATLANTIC OCEAN, R. Shannon, IRELAND, Carrauntoohil 1041 m, Cork)

Ireland is in northern **Europe**.
The north-east corner of the island
is called Northern Ireland and it is
part of the United Kingdom.

Ireland has lots of land. Most people live spread out over the country. About one and a half million people live in or around Dublin, the **capital**.

Land

The centre of Ireland is low, flat farmland and **bog**. There are mountains around the coast. These beautiful, rounded mountains are not very high.

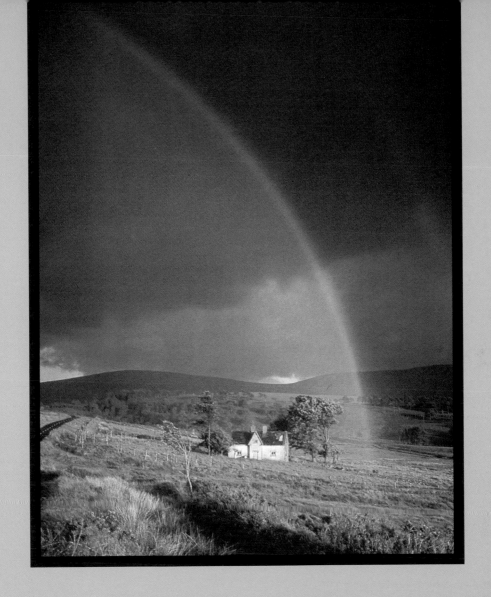

The land looks green all year round
because it has so much rain. Winds bring
clouds from the Atlantic Ocean. These
drop rain as soon as they reach Ireland.

Landmarks

There are many **ancient** graves around
Ireland. The most famous one is at Newgrange.
It is over 4000 years old. Sunlight only
reaches inside it on 21 December.

The Burren is in the west of Ireland. It is
a huge, windswept area of rock with
underground caves. There is nowhere else
like it in all of **Europe**.

Homes

There are still a few **traditional** cottages.
These are built from stone and have just
one room. They have **thatched** roofs
and a plot of land for growing food.

About 150 years ago, cruel landowners forced most people to move off their land to towns or overseas. Today many people live in modern houses in towns.

Food

Irish people usually eat their main
meal at lunchtime. It might be Dublin
coddle, a stew of sausages, bacon,
onions and potatoes.

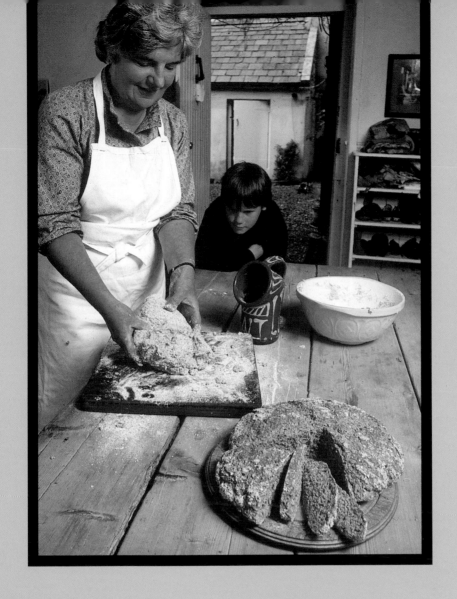

Traditionally, Ireland makes a lot of different breads and potato dishes, and the **dairies** make very good cheeses. There is also lots of fresh seafood.

Clothes

Ireland is famous for its **textiles**. Sheep provide wool which is woven into beautiful clothes. You can still buy handmade Aran jumpers from Galway, or beautiful **tweed** from Donegal.

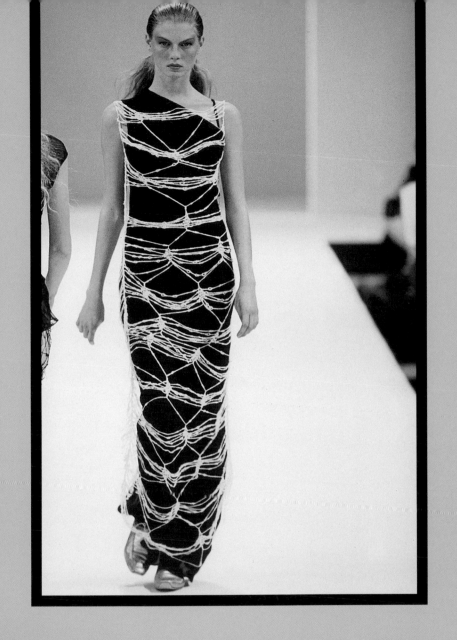

In the last few years, some top **fashion designers** have moved to Dublin. Business is good for new designers and shops.

Work

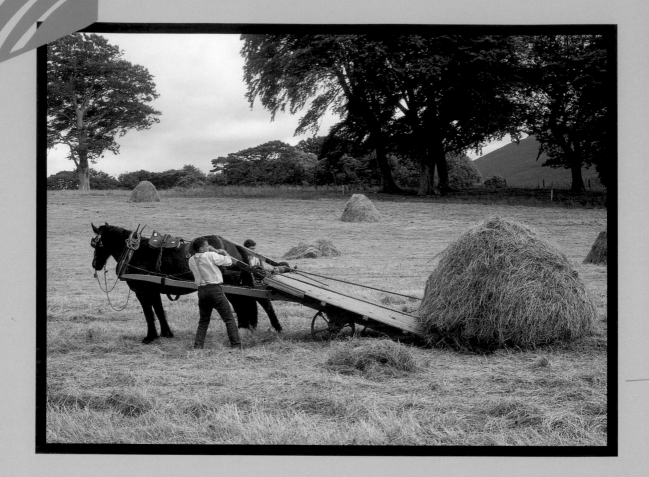

Many farms are still small and people grow just enough food for themselves. In the west, there are beef and **dairy** farms. **Crops** grow better in the east, where it is not so wet.

Many people work in factories, making food or drink, like Guinness, the famous Irish beer. Glass, computers, metals, chemicals and **textiles** are also made.

Transport

It is easy to travel to and from other parts of **Europe** by both sea and air. Ireland has three **international** airports, and its own airline, Aer Lingus.

Almost all travel within Ireland is by road. There is also the Dart, a train route on part of the east coast.

language

English and Irish are the two **official** languages of Ireland. The Irish language was brought to Ireland about 2000 years ago by people from Eastern **Europe**.

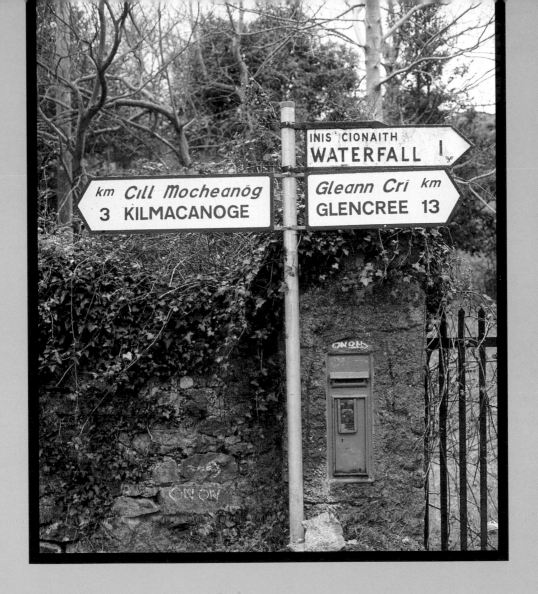

Everyone learns Irish at school, and road signs are written in English and Irish. Some people in the west of Ireland still speak Irish as their main language.

School

Children go to primary school between the ages of six and twelve. The day starts at nine in the morning and finishes at about three in the afternoon.

Students have to go to secondary school from the age of 12 to 15. Their days are longer and they have more homework.

Free time

Many Irish people enjoy watching or playing sport. Race meetings attract huge crowds and many young people keep their own ponies, even in the cities!

On Sunday, some families watch their
local teams play **traditional** games.
Hurling is a fast game played with a
stick and ball. In **Gaelic** football, the
players are allowed to hold the ball.

Celebrations

The Irish Derby at Kildare is held in June.
It is an important day for many Irish
people and horses from all around the
world take part in the race.

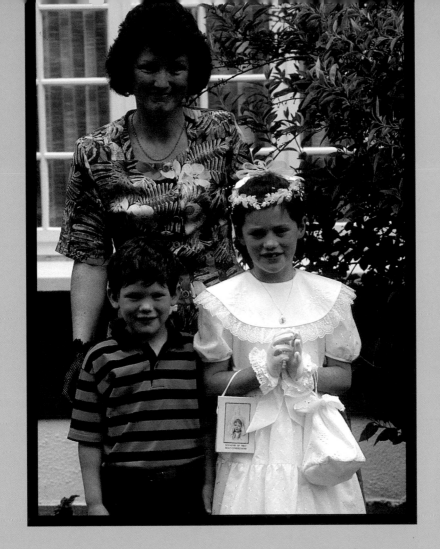

A special day for every **Catholic** child is their First **Communion**. Everyone goes to church in their best clothes. Each child chooses a saint's name to add to their own.

The Arts

Long ago, each Irish village had its own storyteller. Some of their stories were written down in beautiful books. Ireland has produced many famous writers.

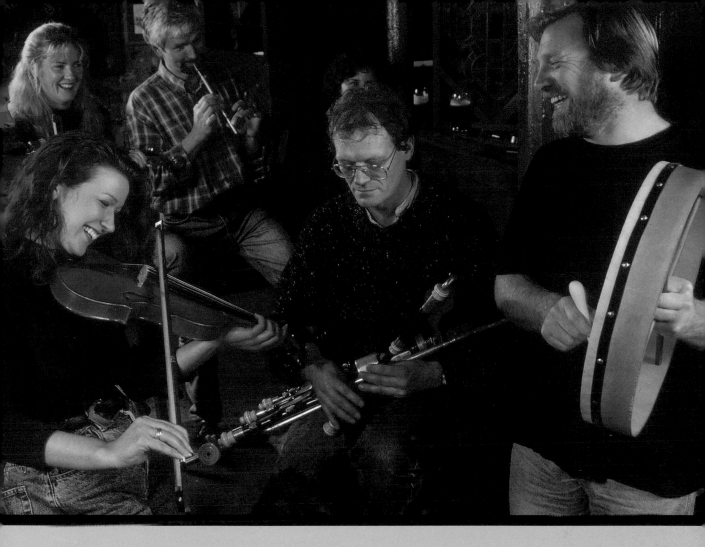

Almost every village has a **traditional** music group. People play the fiddle, the tin whistle, the uileann pipes and the bodhrán (a small goatskin drum). They play dance tunes and old **Gaelic** songs.

Factfile

Name	The full name of Ireland is the Republic of Ireland.
Capital	The **capital** city is Dublin.
Language	**Gaelic** Irish and English are the two **official** languages of Ireland.
Population	There are about three and a half million people living in Ireland.
Money	The Irish have the Irish pound or punt (IR£) which is divided into 100 pence.
Religion	Almost all Irish people are **Catholics**. About three out of 100 people are **Protestant**.
Products	Ireland produces wheat, barley, potatoes, milk, **livestock**, beer, machinery and transport equipment.

Words you can learn

aon (ayn)	one
dó (doe)	two
trí (three)	three
tá (thaw)	yes
níl (knee)	no
dia dhuit (dee-a-gwit)	hello
slán agat (slawn-aguth)	goodbye
le do thoil (le-do-hull)	please

Glossary

ancient	from a long time ago
bog	land that is always wet and spongy
capital	the city where the government is based
Catholic	Christians who have the Pope in Rome as the head of their Church
Communion	the Christian ceremony of eating bread and wine
crops	the plants that farmers grow and harvest (gather)
dairies/dairy	the type of farm that produces milk, cheese and yoghurt
Europe	the collection of countries north of the Mediterranean Sea
fashion designers	people who draw ideas for, and make, clothes
Gaelic	the **ancient** language of the people who first lived in Ireland, Wales and Breton, or describing anything that belonged to them
international	to do with countries all around the World, not just Ireland
livestock	animals kept on a farm for their meat or milk
official	decided by the government
Protestant	Christians who do not have the Pope as the head of their Church
textiles	cloths or fabrics
thatched	roofs made from thick layers of straw or reeds
traditional	the way things have been done or made for a long time
tweed	a thick, woven, wool fabric

Index